# This is our Planet

Written by Rob Alcraft

**Collins**

Our planet is full of life.
You can find life in all kinds
of environments.

desert environment

hot

2

Arctic environment

freezing

3

# Sunshine and heat

Big parts of our planet are desert. Life is difficult in this hot and hostile environment.

camel riders

Deserts can be roasting hot in the day, and freezing at night!

# Wild forest

Wild forests are important environments for our planet.

Wildlife can hide and feed in the trees.

squirrel

little owl

# High peaks

Lines of peaks reach up high.
On steep hillsides, you might spot kites hunting for food.

Ibexes are wild goats that can survive high up.

# Wide plains

These rolling plains go on for miles.
Lions hunt and herds of zebras graze here.

The name for a pack of lions is a pride.

# Arctic chill

In the Arctic, it might seem bleak and hostile. But you can still find living things that survive here.

Arctic fox

sea otter

seal

13

# Fields

Just a tenth of our planet is farmland.

But so much food comes from fertile fields like these.

combine harvester

## Coast and beach

You can find lots of houses on the hillsides and along the coastline.

People like to travel and fish from boats on the sea.

# Town

Towns are important for people's lives.
People drive cars, or ride on buses and trains.

Towns are perfect for shopping, playing and jobs of all kinds.

tram

# We have just one planet

We must keep our planet and all its environments safe.

# Environments on our planet

# 🐾 Review: After reading 🐾

Use your assessment from hearing the children read to choose any GPCs, words or tricky words that need additional practice.

## Read 1: Decoding

- Focus on the /ee/ and /igh/ sounds.
- Look together at pages 12 and 13. Challenge the children to find two words in which the /ee/ sound is written differently. (*seem; bleak, sea, seal*) Turn to page 15. Can the children find the /ee/ sound written differently? (*fields*)
- Ask the children to read these words, and then identify the letter or letters that make the /igh/ sound.

  ibexes     hillsides     coastline     kinds

## Read 2: Prosody

- Model reading each page with expression to the children. After you have read each page, ask the children to have a go at reading with expression.
- On pages 2 and 3 show the children how you point to the labelled images as you read the labels.

## Read 3: Comprehension

- Turn to pages 22 and 23 and ask the children to think of a caption for each photo.
- For every question ask the children how they know the answer. Ask:
  o Which environment can be very hot and very cold? (*desert*)
  o What is the name for a pack of lions? (*a pride*)
  o On pages 12 and 13, who might find the Arctic environment "bleak and hostile"? (e.g. *human beings and lots of animals and birds*)
  o How do you think the author feels about our planet? Why?